HAL LEONARD

GUITAR METHOD
Supplement to Any Guitar Method

CLASSICAL GUITAR PIECES

24 Pieces Arranged for Solo Classical

BY PAUL HENRY

To access audio visit:
www.halleonard.com/mylibrary

Enter Code
2904-9943-6030-6613

ISBN 978-1-4234-3220-3

HAL•LEONARD®
7777 W. BLUEMOUND RD. P.O. BOX 13819 MILWAUKEE, WI 53213

In Australia Contact:
Hal Leonard Australia Pty. Ltd.
4 Lentara Court
Cheltenham, Victoria, 3192 Australia
Email: ausadmin@halleonard.com.au

Visit Hal Leonard Online at
www.halleonard.com

This collection of pieces for the classical guitar is intended for the serious if not yet advanced player as an introduction to the wealth of diverse and beautiful music that is available to guitarists. The selections are comprised of several different styles, time periods, and composers from numerous regions around the world. It is hoped that the accompanying audio recordings will provide inspiration and musical direction. However, as you play these pieces be sure to explore and find the expression and nuances that make the music come alive for you.

– Paul Henry

CONTENTS

ANDANTE

TRACK 1

Matteo Carcassi
(1792-1853)

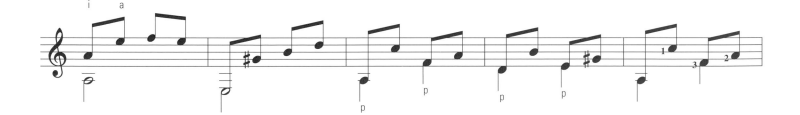

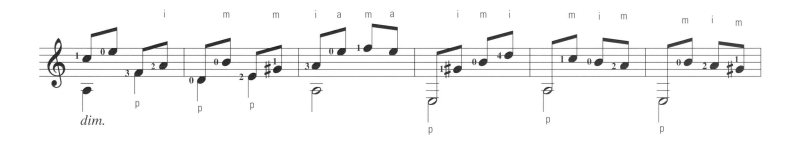

ESTUDIO IN C

TRACK 2

Fernando Sor
(1778-1839)

5

ALLEGRO IN A MINOR

Mauro Giuliani
(1781-1829)

To Coda ⊕

D.C. al Coda

⊕ **Coda**

THE REAPER

TRACK 4

Francois Couperin
(1668-1733)

*2nd time, **p***

rit.

DANCE FOR LUTE

TRACK 5

Drop D tuning:
(low to high) D-A-D-G-B-E

G.L. Fuhrmann
from Testudo-Gallo Germanica 1615

CANCION I

TRACK 6

Spanish Traditional

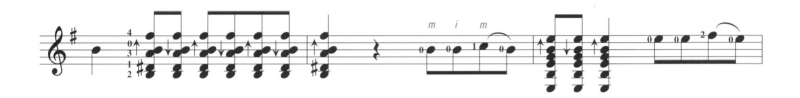

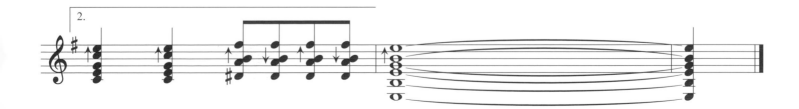

CANCION II

TRACK 7

Spanish Traditional

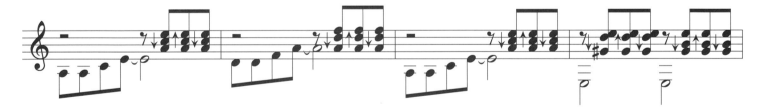

SIMPLE GIFTS

TRACK 8

American Traditional

11

ALLEGRO

TRACK 9

W.A. Mozart
(1756-1791)

poco rit.

12

ANDANTE IN C

TRACK 10

Fernando Sor
(1778-1839)

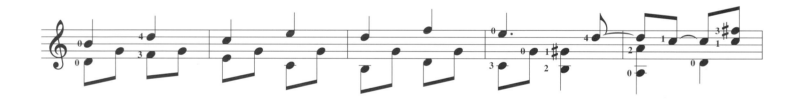

CATALAN FOLK SONG

TRACK 11

Anonymous

Espressivo

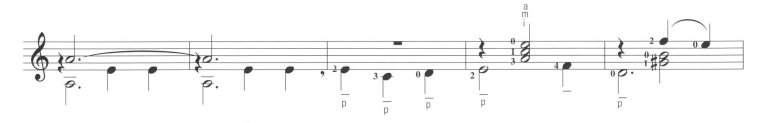

Molto espresivo

rit.

MENUETT

TRACK 12

Johann Kreiger
(1651-1735)

GAVOTTE

TRACK 13

G.P. Telemann
(1681-1767)

16

Copyright © 2008 by HAL LEONARD CORPORATION
International Copyright Secured   All Rights Reserved

CARAVAN

TRACK 14

Iberian Traditional

KEMP'S JIG

TRACK 15

Anonymous
English Folk Song

18

ALLEGRETTO OP. 30

Mauro Giuliani
(1781-1829)

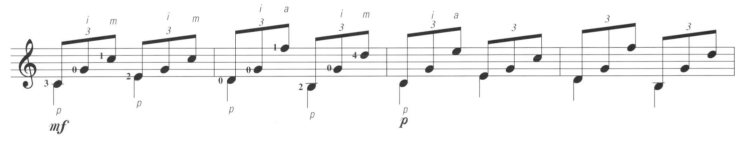

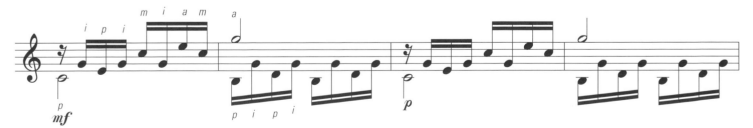

ANDANTINO IN A MINOR

TRACK 16

Fernando Carulli
(1770-1841)

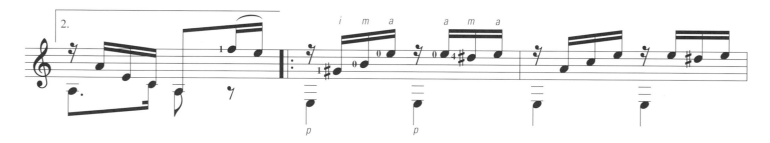

D.S. al Coda
(take 2nd ending)

⊕ **Coda**

rit.

SCARBOROUGH FAIR

English Traditional

rit.

22

ESTUDIO IN E MINOR

Fernando Sor
(1778-1839)

23

ORLANDO SLEEPETH

John Dowland
(1563-1626)

ALLEGRETTO

TRACK 21

Fernando Carulli
(1770-1841)

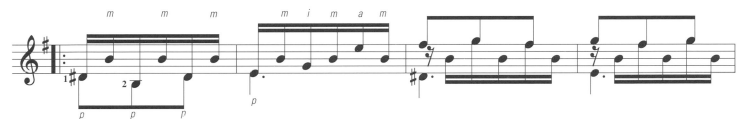

Fine

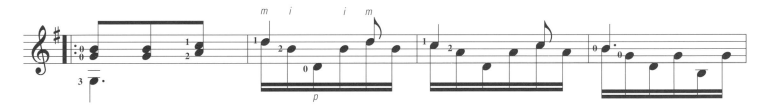

2nd time, D.C. al Fine
(no repeats)

25

PASTORALE

TRACK 22

Matteo Carcassi
(1792-1853)

JESU, JOY OF MAN'S DESIRING

J.S. Bach
(1685-1750)

poco rit.

BOURREE

G.F. Handel
(1685-1759)

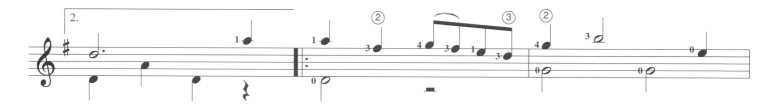

CLASSICAL GUITAR

INSTRUCTIONAL BOOKS & METHODS AVAILABLE FROM HAL LEONARD

CLASSICAL STUDIES FOR PICK-STYLE GUITAR

by William Leavitt
Berklee Press

This Berklee Workshop, featuring over 20 solos and duets by Bach, Carcassi, Paganini, Sor and other renowned composers, is designed to acquaint intermediate to advanced pick-style guitarists with some of the excellent classical music that is adaptable to pick-style guitar. With study and practice, this workshop will increase a player's knowledge and proficiency on this formidable instrument.
50449440..............................$14.99

ÉTUDES SIMPLES FOR GUITAR

by Leo Brouwer
Editions Max Eschig

This new, completely revised and updated edition includes critical commentary and performance notes. Each study is accompanied by an introduction that illustrates its principal musical features and technical objectives, complete with suggestions and preparatory exercises.
50565810 Book/CD Pack.....................$26.99

FIRST BOOK FOR THE GUITAR

by Frederick Noad
G. Schirmer, Inc.

A beginner's manual to the classical guitar. Uses a systematic approach using the interesting solo and duet music written by Noad, one of the world's foremost guitar educators. No musical knowledge is necessary. Student can progress by simple stages. Many of the exercises are designed for a teacher to play with the students. Will increase student's enthusiasm, therefore increasing the desire to take lessons.
50334370 Part 1......................$12.99
50334520 Part 2......................$18.99
50335160 Part 3......................$16.99
50336760 Complete Edition...................$32.99

HAL LEONARD CLASSICAL GUITAR METHOD

by Paul Henry

This comprehensive and easy-to-use beginner's guide uses the music of the master composers to teach you the basics of the classical style and technique. Includes pieces by Beethoven, Bach, Mozart, Schumann, Giuliani, Carcassi, Bathioli, Aguado, Tarrega, Purcell, and more. Includes all the basics plus info on PIMA technique, two- and three-part music, time signatures, key signatures, articulation, free stroke, rest stroke, composers, and much more.
00697376 Book/Online Audio (no tab) $16.99
00142652 Book/Online Audio (with tab) $17.99

A MODERN APPROACH TO CLASSICAL GUITAR

by Charles Duncan

This multi-volume method was developed to allow students to study the art of classical guitar within a new, more contemporary framework. For private, class or self-instruction.

00695114 Book 1 – Book Only.............................$8.99
00695113 Book 1 – Book/Online Audio................$12.99
00699204 Book 1 – Repertoire Book Only...........$11.99
00699205 Book 1 – Repertoire Book/Online Audio . $16.99
00695116 Book 2 – Book Only.............................$8.99
00695115 Book 2 – Book/Online Audio................$12.99
00699208 Book 2 – Repertoire...........................$12.99
00699202 Book 3 – Book Only.............................$9.99
00695117 Book 3 – Book/Online Audio...............$14.99
00695119 Composite Book/CD Pack....................$32.99

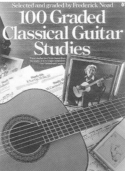

100 GRADED CLASSICAL GUITAR STUDIES

Selected and Graded by Frederick Noad

Frederick Noad has selected 100 studies from the works of three outstanding composers of the classical period: Sor, Giuliani, and Carcassi. All these studies are invaluable for developing both right hand and left hand skills. Students and teachers will find this book invaluable for making technical progress. In addition, they will build a repertoire of some of the most melodious music ever written for the guitar.
14023154...$29.99

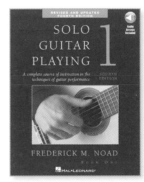

CHRISTOPHER PARKENING GUITAR METHOD

THE ART & TECHNIQUE OF THE CLASSICAL GUITAR

Guitarists will learn basic classical technique by playing over 50 beautiful classical pieces, 26 exercises and 14 duets, and through numerous photos and illustrations. The method covers: rudiments of classical technique, note reading and music theory, selection and care of guitars, strategies for effective practicing, and much more!
00696023 Book 1/Online Audio $22.99
00695228 Book 1 (No Audio) $17.99
00696024 Book 2/Online Audio $22.99
00695229 Book 2 (No Audio) $17.99

SOLO GUITAR PLAYING

by Frederick M. Noad

Solo Guitar Playing can teach even the person with no previous musical training how to progress from simple single-line melodies to mastery of the guitar as a solo instrument. Fully illustrated with diagrams, photographs, and over 200 musical exercises and repertoire selections, these books offer instruction in every phase of classical guitar playing.
14023147 Book 1/Online Audio $34.99
14023153 Book 1 (Book Only) $24.99
14023151 Book 2 (Book Only) $19.99

TWENTY STUDIES FOR THE GUITAR

ANDRÉS SEGOVIA EDITION

by Fernando Sor
Performed by Paul Henry

20 studies for the classical guitar written by Beethoven's contemporary, Fernando Sor, revised, edited and fingered by the great classical guitarist Andres Segovia. These essential repertoire pieces continue to be used by teachers and students to build solid classical technique. Features 50-minute demonstration audio.
00695012 Book/Online Audio $22.99
00006363 Book Only..$9.99

Prices, contents and availability subject to change without notice.

THE PUBLICATIONS OF
CHRISTOPHER PARKENING

CHRISTOPHER PARKENING – DUETS AND CONCERTOS

Throughout his career, Christopher Parkening has had the opportunity to perform with many of the world's leading artists and orchestras, and this folio contains many selections from those collaborations. All of the pieces included here have been edited and fingered for the guitar by Christopher Parkening himself.
00690938..$24.99

THE CHRISTOPHER PARKENING GUITAR METHOD, VOL. 1 – REVISED

in collaboration with
Jack Marshall and David Brandon

Learn the art of the classical guitar with this premier method for beginners by one of the world's preeminent virtuosos and the recognized heir to the legacy of Andrés Segovia. Learn basic classical guitar technique by playing beautiful pieces of music, including over 50 classical pieces, 26 exercises, and 14 duets. Includes notes in the first position, how to hold the guitar, tuning, right and left hand technique, arpeggios, tone production, placement of fingers and nails, flats, naturals, key signatures, the bar, and more. Also includes many helpful photos and illustrations, plus sections on the history of the classical guitar, selecting a guitar, guitar care, and more.
00695228 Book...$14.99
00696023 Book/Online Audio $22.99

THE CHRISTOPHER PARKENING GUITAR METHOD, VOL. 2

Intermediate to Upper-Intermediate Level

Continues where Vol. 1 leaves off. Teaches: all notes in the upper position; tone production; advanced techniques such as tremolo, harmonics, vibrato, pizzicato and slurs; practice tips; stylistic interpretation; and more. The first half of the book deals primarily with technique, while the second half of the book applies the technique with repertoire pieces. As a special bonus, this book includes 32 previously unpublished Parkening edition pieces by composers including Dowland, Bach, Scarlatti, Sor, Tarrega and other, plus three duets for two guitars.
00695229 Book...$14.99
00696024 Book/Online Audio $22.99

PARKENING AND THE GUITAR – VOL. 1

Music of Two Centuries:
Popular New Transcriptions for Guitar
Virtuoso Music for Guitar

Ten transcriptions for solo guitar of beautiful music from many periods and styles, edited and fingered by Christopher Parkening. All pieces are suitable for performance by the advanced guitarist. Ten selections: Afro-Cuban Lullaby • Empress of the Pagodes (Ravel) • Menuet (Ravel) • Minuet in D (Handel) • Passacaille (Weiss) • Pastourelle (Poulenc) • Pavane for a Dead Princess (Ravel) • Pavane for a Sleeping Beauty (Ravel) • Preambulo (Scarlatti-Ponce) • Sarabande (Handel).
00699105..$9.95

PARKENING AND THE GUITAR – VOL. 2

Music of Two Centuries:
Popular New Transcriptions for Guitar
Virtuoso Music for Guitar

Nine more selections for the advanced guitarist: Clair de Lune (Debussy) • Giga (Visée) • The Girl with the Flaxen Hair (Debussy) • Gymnopedie Nos. I-III (Satie) • The Little Shepherd (Debussy) • The Mysterious Barricades (Couperin) • Sarabande (Debussy).
00699106..$9.95

CHRISTOPHER PARKENING – ROMANZA

Virtuoso Music for Guitar

Three wonderful transcriptions edited and fingered by Parkening: Catalonian Song • Rumores de la Caleta • Romance.
00699103..$10.99

CHRISTOPHER PARKENING – SACRED MUSIC FOR THE GUITAR, VOL. 1

Seven inspirational arrangements, transcriptions and compositions covering traditional Christian melodies from several centuries. These selections appear on the Parkening album Sacred Music for the Guitar. Includes: Präludium (Bach) • Our Great Savior • God of Grace and God of Glory (2 guitars) • Brethren, We Have Met to Worship • Deep River • Jesus, We Want to Meet • Evening Prayer.
00699095..$14.99

CHRISTOPHER PARKENING – SACRED MUSIC FOR THE GUITAR, VOL. 2

Seven more selections from the album *Sacred Music for the Guitar:* Hymn of Christian Joy (guitar and harpsichord) • Simple Gifts • Fairest Lord Jesus • Stir Thy Church, O God Our Father • All Creatures of Our God and King • Glorious Things of Thee Are Spoken • Praise Ye the Lord (2 guitars).
00699100..$15.99

CHRISTOPHER PARKENING – SOLO PIECES

Sixteen transcriptions for solo guitar edited and fingered by Parkening, including: Allegro • Danza • Fugue • Galliard • I Stand at the Threshold • Prelude • Sonata in D • Suite Española • Suite in D Minor • and more.
00690939..$24.99

PARKENING PLAYS BACH

Virtuoso Music for Guitar

Nine transcriptions edited and fingered by Parkening: Preludes I, VI & IX • Gavottes I & II • Jesu, Joy of Man's Desiring • Sheep May Safely Graze • Wachet Auf, Ruft Uns Die Stemme • Be Thou with Me • Sleepers Awake (2 guitars).
00699104..$9.95

CHRISTOPHER PARKENING – VIRTUOSO PERFORMANCES

This DVD features performances and career highlights from classical guitar virtuoso Christopher Parkening (filmed in 1971, 1973, 1998 and 2003). Viewers can watch feature titles in their entirety or select individual songs. As a bonus, there is archival footage of Andrés Segovia performing in studio, circa 1950. The DVD also includes an informational booklet. 95 minutes.
00320506 DVD $24.99

HAL•LEONARD®

www.halleonard.com